The Prestige Series

CW00493489

United Co

John Banks

© 2005 Venture Publications Ltd

ISBN 1 898432 49 X

All rights reserved. Except for normal review purposes no part of this book may be reproduced or utilised in any form or by any means, electrical or mechanical, including photocopying, recording or by an information storage and retrieval system, without the prior written consent of Venture Publications Ltd, Glossop, Derbyshire.

Cover: Lines of new buses outside the Eastern Coach Works factory in Lowestoft, awaiting delivery to their owners, were for so long a sight to gladden the eye of the enthusiast. On this occasion in 1978 United Counties Bristol VR No. **902** (**CBD 902T**) was at the head of the queue. *(Geoff Coxon)*

Rear cover: The United Counties timetable for September 1960 boasted a colourful cover and a bargain price of one shilling - not bad for 348 pages of densely packed information and two maps, not to mention the county shields and the Bristol Lodekka on the front. *(John Banks Collection)*

Inside covers: A cross-section of what was running on United Counties stage-carriage services right on the change from Transport Holding Company to National Bus Company control. Liveries are much the same, save for the suppression of the upper cream band on the double-deckers. These pictures were taken in Stamford - No. **121** (**PNV 221**) - and Biggleswade on 8th August 1969. Noteable among the standard Bristol/ECW stock is No. **489** (**MAX 109**), a 1954 LS6G 45-seater that had come from Red and White Services, of Chepstow, in 1968. The movement of vehicles among the constituents of the NBC was to become very common. *(All: John Banks)*

Title page: In the thirties the United Counties fleet was rather mixed, mainly as the result of acquired operators' fleets. New vehicles in that period, however, were often purchased from Leyland Motors Ltd, including No. **405** (**VV 3775**), a splendid Eastern Counties-bodied 30-seat rear-entrance coach dating from 1935. The chassis was a Leyland Tiger TS7 and the vehicle ran for United Counties until 1951. *(Ron Maybray Collection)*

Opposite page: Number **625** (**GP 6241**) was a 1931 Thomas Tilling AEC Regent that had come to United Counties from the Brighton, Hove & District Omnibus Co. Ltd in the dark days of 1943. Originally fitted with an outside-staircase highbridge body of Tilling's own manufacture, it received this Eastern Coach Works 53-seat lowbridge replacement in 1944. The photograph was taken in June 1948. *(Alan Cross Collection)*

Below: As was to be expected in a Tilling fleet, the second half of the fifties and the following decade saw the arrival of many Bristol Lodekkas. The centre of this trio is one of the earliest: No. **958** (**JBD 963**) was a 1954 LD6B (and therefore Bristol-engined) model with Eastern Coach Works 58-seat bodywork with platform doors. The flanking vehicles - Nos **517** and **527** (**NBD 916/ORP 27**) - were similar in most respects save for seating 60; they dated from 1957. *(Ron Maybray Collection)*

INTRODUCTION

The Wellingborough Motor Omnibus Company Limited

The United Counties Omnibus and Road Transport Company Limited came into being in 1921, but its roots go back at least a further nine years, to 1912 and the commencement of operations in Bedford by Mr W B Richardson's New Central Omnibus Company Limited. That led to the foundation in 1913 of the Wellingborough Motor Omnibus Company Limited, which in turn, in 1921, became the United Counties that is the subject of this book.

There is an oft-repeated, and possibly apocryphal, story that one of Mr Richardson's Bedford crews had the bright idea of hiring one of their employer's buses, allegedly for private hire work, and running it in service in Wellingborough - and successfully, at that.

WBR, upon hearing of this, despatched one of his officials to follow the bus and report on its crew's activities. True or not, something drew his attention to Wellingborough and he started a circular service out from and back to Wellingborough via Finedon, Irthlingborough, Higham Ferrers and Rushden. Results were encouraging and Richardson put a second bus on, working the same route in the opposite direction. Thus was born the Wellingborough Motor Omnibus Company Limited.

The Wellingborough company used Leylands in some quantities and when the operation was sold to the new United Counties in 1921, no fewer than 37 "in running order" were transferred, as well as a further two under construction at the time of the sale.

The United Counties Omnibus & Road Transport Company Limited

Although this was a genuine sale, followed by the official winding up of the Wellingborough company, the United Counties operation kept its head office in Wellingborough and its daily operations based on Irthlingborough, exactly as had the earlier operator and to the public very little seemed to have changed apart from the name on the sides of the buses.

At the time of the formation of United Counties, seven routes were in operation:

1. Wellingborough to Rushden
2. Irthlingborough to Northampton
3. Rushden to Desborough
4. Wellingborough to Raunds
5. Wellingborough to Wollaston
6. Kettering to Northampton
7. Wellingborough to Kettering

An interesting and unusual arrangement regarding the acquisition of new vehicles involved the Company buying them from Managing Director W B Richardson, who had bought them from Leyland Motors in, it seems, some sort of capacity as a dealer. Certainly he made a profit on each sale. The first order from the Company to Richardson under this arrangement called for twelve RAF-type chassis to be delivered in 1922, upon which the Company built its own bodywork; eleven were 52-seaters and the other had 60 seats - a remarkable capacity for the era.

Soon afterwards further Leylands were bought under a similar arrangement, but this time the "dealer" was the Company's engineer, Walter Crook. This was the same Crook who, later in 1922, was one of the two founders of the City Motor Omnibus Company in London.

In those early days there was some modest extension to services as thought remunerative and a new route, numbered 8, was put on between Kettering and Geddington in 1923. In the mid 1920s much effort was put into rebodying older vehicles and purchases of new Leylands continued.

A new depot was opened at Desborough in 1925, permitting the introduction of two new services from that town, the 9 to Market Harborough and the 9A to Kettering. On the vehicle side, 1925 was noteworthy for the arrival of the first pneumatic-tyred buses - again Leylands.

W B Richardson died in 1927; he was replaced by J J Johnson, one of whose first acts was to preside over the delivery of 18 Leyland Lions (of type PLSC3 - known unofficially at Leyland as the "Long" Lion), bodied either by Christopher Dodson, of Willesden, or Short Brothers, of Rochester (acting as sub-contractors to Leyland Motors). The addition of the Lions and six second-hand RAF Leylands from United Automobile Services pushed the fleet total to almost 100 by the end of 1927.

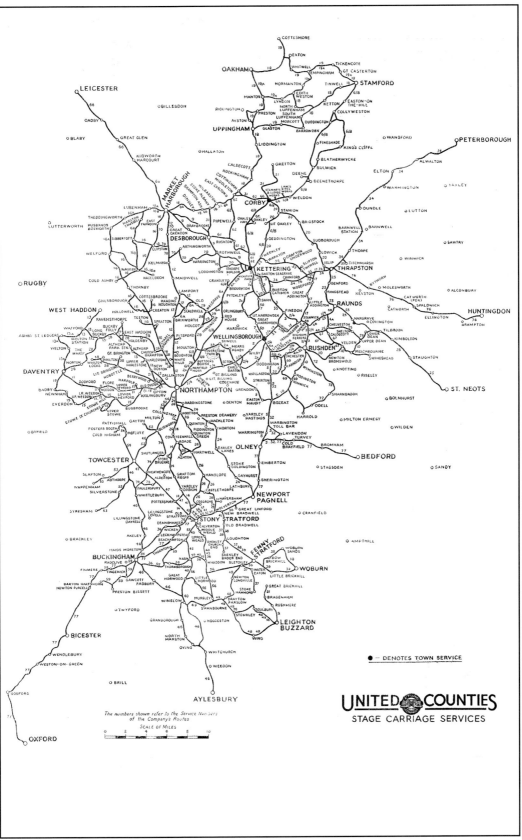

UNITED COUNTIES
STAGE CARRIAGE SERVICES

5

The United Counties Omnibus & Road Transport Company never operated as freight hauliers; that it had intended to is hinted at only in a bit of negative evidence: the new Desborough depot did not occupy all the land purchased for it and in 1927 the unused portion was sold. It has been suggested that this land had been meant to house the road haulage side of the business.

By this time the Company was sufficiently well established and mature to enter into territorial agreements with three adjacent large operators: the Peterborough Electric Traction Company Limited (in 1931 to form part of the new Eastern Counties operation), the National Omnibus & Transport Company Limited and Midland Red. Before the agreement, United Counties had not got on too well with Midland Red in the 1920s, the latter having attempted to start services in Northampton on two separate occasions. Matters were brought to a head at the end of the decade (*after* the agreement, be it noted) when United Counties retaliated to Midland Red's application for a Leicester to Northampton service by applying for some routes in Leicester.

Like many others among those operators that survived to become large company operators in post-Second World War Britain, United Counties was a voracious acquirer of competing businesses, no fewer than 33 joining the fold between 1921 and 1933. The policy of standardising on Leylands took a bit of a battering through those acquisitions: Bedford, Chevrolet, Commer, Daimler, Dennis, Federal, GMC, Gilford, Lancia, Maudslay, Reo, Star, Thornycroft and Tilling-Stevens were among the makes acquired.

As the Company entered its second decade it had a fleet of 136 buses garaged at Irthlingborough (55), Northampton (39), Desborough (25) and Kettering (13). Outstation stabling arrangements were in force at Stony Stratford, Daventry and Stamford for the remaining four vehicles. The Company's preference for Leylands continued and in 1930 the first Lions of the improved LT1 type appeared, as did the first Titans; there were seven of the latter, ordered after satisfactory performance from a TD1 demonstrator, which was retained, in late 1929. Whereas the latter had an open staircase, the 1930 TD1s were to the more modern and safer enclosed-staircase design.

A momentous change followed an approach from the London, Midland & Scottish Railway in May 1929. Negotiations with the LMS dragged on unsatisfactorily for almost two years and came to naught, but in March 1931 further discussion was pre-empted by an offer from Thomas Tilling Limited to buy all the United Counties shares. By the July it was all over, with a Tilling nominee joining the United Counties Board. The Company remained most unusual among those in which Tilling took an interest in that the railways at no time managed to acquire any influence.

In 1931 and 1932 the Leyland Titan increased its presence in the fleet - the later examples were of the improved TD2 type.

The Company moved its registered office to Irthlingborough in June 1933; by the autumn of that year route numbers had reached 35 and there was leisure traffic, mainly worked by the Leyland Lion single-deckers, to such places as Clacton, Great Yarmouth and Whipsnade Zoo.

In September 1933 the name of the Company was changed to United Counties Omnibus Company Limited, often shortened in writing, and sometimes even in speech, to "UCOC".

The United Counties Omnibus Company Limited

The new Company had, on its inception day, 20th September 1933, a fleet of 154 public service vehicles (105 single- and 49 double-deck). Up to then the United Counties livery had been blue and white with red wheels; it was now changed to green and cream.

As an indirect result of the forthcoming formation of the London Passenger Transport Board in 1933, the Aylesbury Omnibus Company was taken over by Eastern National in May of that year in a complicated manoeuvre, which eventually saw United Counties, on 1st December of that year, acquiring those Aylesbury services in its area along with four vehicles. At the same time, Eastern National's Stony Stratford section was transferred to United Counties. This was a combined boost to the Company's operations of 15 routes. The four Aylesbury vehicles

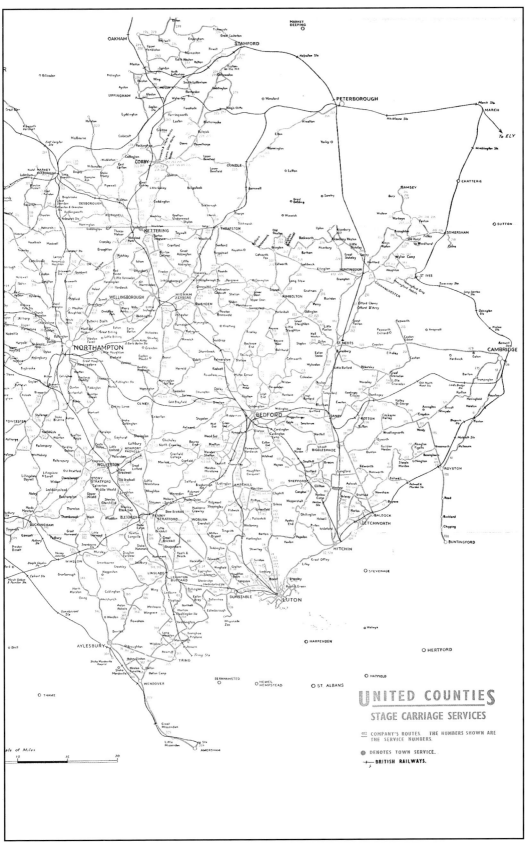

UNITED COUNTIES

STAGE CARRIAGE SERVICES

402 COMPANY'S ROUTES. THE NUMBERS SHOWN ARE
THE SERVICE NUMBERS.

DENOTES TOWN SERVICE.

BRITISH RAILWAYS.

mentioned above were Leyland Tigers, and in addition Eastern National transferred three Leyland Titans, two Leyland Lions and a pair of ADCs.

Adequately capitalised as it now was under Tilling control, the Company pursued its programme of acquiring other operators' services and vehicles; between October 1933 and the outbreak of the Second World War there were 28 such takeovers. Among the largest were Allchin's Luxury Coaches, of Northampton, with 31 vehicles in December 1933, bringing a substantial network of express coach services; W A Nightingale & Sons, also of Northampton, (16 vehicles in February 1934) and F & E Beeden, again of Northampton, in June 1938, a transaction that brought 18 buses.

One of the oddest acquisitions was the Oxford to London service formerly worked by Varsity Express Motors, of Cambridge. Varsity was taken over by the Eastern Counties Omnibus Company in August 1933. The Oxford service was a long way from its area and so was transferred in April 1934 to the nearest Tilling operator to Oxford, which happened to be United Counties, though even at that the service could not really be said to have been in UCOC territory.

Possession of the ex-Allchin express services led to United Counties, a little later in 1934, becoming one of the founder members of the Associated Motorways network (see "Associated Motorways", by Keith Healey, No. 18 in The Prestige Series, published by Venture Publications Ltd in 2002).

That year - 1934 - was an extremely eventful one, for it also saw the Company's head office moved to Northampton; plans were put in hand for a new bus and coach station in Derngate, Northampton, which was opened for limited use in October 1934 but which was not fully operational until March 1936, after which it was home to all of the Company's bus and coach services.

The mid and late 1930s for United Counties followed the pattern seen in many other companies - that of considerable expansion of both services and fleet. As was to be expected of a Tilling operator, orders for new vehicles moved away from previous suppliers (in this case mainly Leyland) towards Bristol, with J-

and L-type single-deckers and K-type double-deckers entering the fleet up to the outbreak of war and beyond.

The war brought its share of problems, as it did to the rest of the Industry. Some of the Company's buses were requisitioned by the military authorities; a situation somewhat alleviated by second-hand purchases of Brighton, Hove & District AEC Regents and Plymouth Leyland Titans; and borrowed Brighton, Hove & District Dennis Lances, AEC Regents and Bristols to a total of 13 and three London Transport STs. New Guy Arab and Bristol utility double-deckers arrived in penny numbers, but these were too few for the Company's needs, judged by peacetime standards, and there was much rebodying and rebuilding of vehicles that would, under normal circumstances, have been withdrawn from service.

Although one wag of a silly-season journalist "reported" that the Dennis Lances, being seaside buses, required passengers to have "sea legs", probably the only difference noticed by passengers was the livery. Much more noticeable, doubtless, were the 15 producer-gas-powered buses because of the anthracite burning apparatus mounted on a two-wheeled trailer they were obliged to tow around. Such vehicles were poor performers and, as in many another company obliged by government decree to use them, officials found that they could not keep to schedule; their use, however, was claimed by the Company to have saved 61,000 gallons of petrol. A further very evident change wrought by the war was the interior conversion of many single-deckers to an arrangement of perimeter seating, which allowed more standing room.

The face of the Company's services also changed during the war, the suspension of all express services in 1942 and troop movements being two among the more obvious to the onlooker.

The Lowestoft premises of Eastern Coach Works were deemed unsafe from potential enemy invasion, and in 1940 ECW rented, later buying, the United Counties Irthlingborough depot.

The war ended in 1945, but for much of the rest of the decade its effects continued to be felt in the form of shortages and rationing. Even

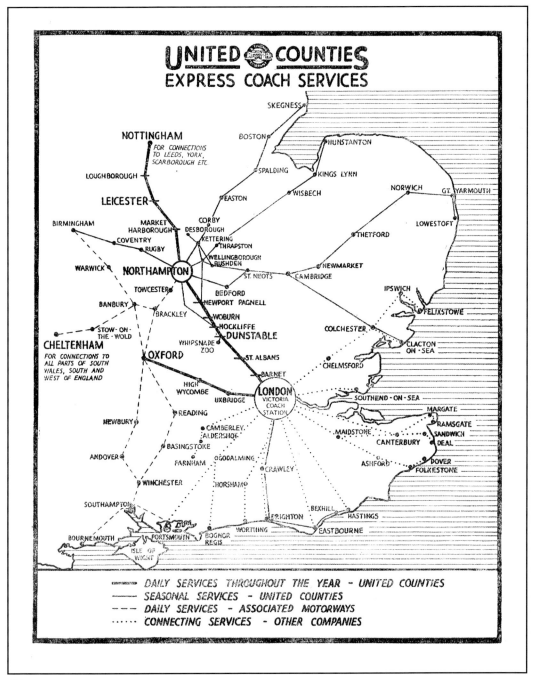

Maps

The map on page 5 shows the extent of the United Counties stage-carriage network in the summer of 1948, that is to say before the Eastern National transfer. With Kettering, Wellingborough, Northampton and Stony Stratford forming a sound core, there was very little to the east of an arc from Stamford to Leighton Buzzard. Page 7, in a map from 1960, shows how the eastern half expanded considerably following the addition of the former Eastern National services.

The express coach services from the summer of 1948 are shown on this page. Although outwardly impressive, the map shows only Nottingham - Northampton - London and Oxford - London as regular United Counties-operated services. (All: John Banks Collection)

9

when new vehicles were built, they often did not go to hard-pressed provincial operators. The priority was export, a situation borne patriotically by most, but it must have felt like insult added wilfully to injury when eight brand new Eastern Coach Works Bristol K double-deckers were diverted to London Transport, where they spent over a year.

The period of austerity was followed by something of a boom in bus usage. United Counties, in its guise as a green Tilling fleet, settled down to cope with this by taking in a typical selection of Eastern Coach Works-bodied Bristol service buses (single- and double-deck) and coaches. The supremacy of Bristol was challenged only by small intakes of Bedford OB and Beadle-Morris single-deckers.

In 1948, along with the other Tilling companies, United Counties passed into the control of the British Transport Commission. It is perhaps worth mentioning that, contrary to an oft-held misconception, the Tilling companies were not "nationalised": they became state-owned through voluntary sale to the Government - an important distinction. The only bus companies to be truly nationalised were the Balfour Beatty group's Midland General, Notts and Derby, and Mansfield District, which were swept into enforced state ownership on the tide of the nationalisation of the electricity industry, in which Balfour Beatty was heavily involved.

On 1st May 1952, the BTC's Tilling Group Management Committee detached the Oxford depot, the Oxford to London express service, and eight coaches, from United Counties and transferred them to South Midland Motor Services Ltd, which was a subsidiary of the Thames Valley Traction Company. This loss was more than compensated, on the same date, by the transfer to United Counties of the Midland Area of the Eastern National Omnibus Company Limited. The 121 routes, eight depots and 247 vehicles involved almost doubled the size of the Company. Eastern National had had a coordination agreement with Luton Corporation since 1932 (amended in 1948). These operations (the revised 1948 agreement came into force on 1st January 1949) were managed by a joint "Luton & District Transport" committee consisting of three members each from the municipality and the

Company. United Counties fell heir to this operation and the two operators worked in harmony until United Counties took over Luton Corporation's bus services in January 1970.

The lists of vehicles transferred leave the peruser with a strong suspicion that Eastern National made sure that more than a fair share of older units were included. It was ever thus: one is reminded of railway shedmasters, when instructed to transfer examples of a certain class of locomotive elsewhere, making very sure that the list included the one in the corner of the yard that would not steam and when it did rode badly, and was invariably refused by any crew allocated to it.

Of the 239 vehicles numbered into the United Counties fleet, Bristols were in the majority, but there were a lot of Leylands - mostly double-deck and mostly prewar - and a few Dennis Lancet single-deckers. Three Bedfords, three Dennises, a Leyland and a Tilling-Stevens, dating from between 1932 and 1939, which were never numbered or, in some cases, used, brought the total to 247.

The Company took the forthcoming influx of Eastern National vehicles as an opportunity to renumber its fleet. Using a simple scheme in which non-PSV stock was numbered up to 99, single-deckers up to 499 and double-deckers from 500, United Counties renumbered its pre-transfer fleet of 297 vehicles on 1st March 1952 and then incorporated the 239 ex-Eastern National vehicles into the same numbering scheme two months later. Few of the prewar vehicles lasted for more than a year or so (some, indeed, were sold almost immediately), but the standard ECW/Bristols fitted in seamlessly and the last ex-Eastern National bus (a 1951 LWL single-decker) was not withdrawn until March 1968.

Although much reduced in comparison with the prewar period, there were some acquisitions of other operators in the fifties and - a sign of the times - problems over coordination when Northampton Corporation sought to extend its provision on the grounds that people had been moved out of the town centre into suburban housing estates and were therefore "theirs"; United Counties riposted that they were already serving the outer fringes perfectly adequately. This was an argument that reverberated repeatedly through meeting- and court-rooms

Above: The Wellingborough Motor Omnibus Co. Ltd relied heavily on Leyland chassis bodied mainly as open-top 36-seat double-deckers. Fleet letter **B** (**LN 329**) is seen on the Northampton to Wellingborough service very early in the First World War (a notice in the bank window announces a "New War Loan").

Below: Fleet letter **H** (**LF 9967**), a similar Leyland, is seen on the Wellingborough to Raunds service, which ran via Rushden, Higham Ferrers and Stanwick - a 58-minute journey. *(Both: John Banks Collection)*

all over the country in that era of postwar housing development.

A look at the miles run and passengers carried in the first twenty years or so of the postwar period is illuminating. In 1949 United Counties ran nearly ten million miles to carry just under 40 million passengers. In the first full year following the Eastern National transfer, 1953, these figures had increased to a fraction under 20 million and just over 92 million respectively. Slight increases saw a peak in 1955 of just over 20 million miles and just over 93½ million passengers, but from there it was all downhill. In 1963 more miles were being run - over 21 million - for a sizeable drop in passengers carried to under 84 million. This - again - was a nationwide picture, and by no means confined to United Counties.

The main reasons for the decline were: increased overall prosperity, which allowed more and more people to afford private motor cars and television sets, so that when they went out at the weekend they did not take the bus, and when they wanted evening entertainment, they stayed in and watched the television, rather than taking the bus to the cinema; and a somewhat blinkered attitude to progress from trade-union influenced platform staff, which resulted in opposition to such economies as driver-only operation and larger vehicles being combined with ever-increasing demands for more pay. It is also undoubtedly true that the bus industry in general could not generate enough revenue to match the wages being paid in other industries, thus adding to their woes the difficulties of attracting and keeping the right calibre of staff.

The National Bus Company

Quite how it was thought that politicians could find a solution where transport professionals had failed is unclear, but nonetheless legislation was passed in 1968 allowing the Transport Holding Company (successors to the British Transport Commission) to acquire the road passenger transport interests of the British Electrical Traction Group and for the formation of the National Bus Company. That is to simplify what actually happened, for the Transport Act, 1968 affected many other areas of transport, including non-THC road

passenger, but it is the part of it that affected United Counties, which on 1st January 1969 became a subsidiary of the National Bus Company, that interests us here.

Not much happened at once, but it was not long before the fruits of the joining of the BET and the THC produced a cooperative vehicle design with the BET's curved windscreen design grafted on to the hitherto flat-fronted ECW designs for Bristol chassis. Visually, things remained much as they had been except for the introduction of a double *N* symbol that looked like an arrow head. This had two versions, for offside and nearside, to ensure that the arrow always pointed forward; at first it was sometimes applied with the arrow pointing the wrong way. The Tilling green of United Counties gave way after a few years to a different, slightly lighter shade of the same colour.

Whether or not the NBC was an unwieldy Leviathan is still a discussion point liable to provoke animated debate. Tacit admission that it might well have been came in the eighties when various companies within it were split into smaller units. United Counties was affected and in September 1985, Managing Director John Tate announced that in the following year the operation would be split into three:

Luton and District, based on Hitchin, Luton, Leighton Buzzard and Aylesbury depots;

Milton Keynes City Bus, based on Milton Keynes depot; and

United Counties, which would be truncated by the loss of those depots and henceforth consist of Northampton, Corby, Kettering, Wellingborough, Bedford, Biggleswade and Huntingdon depots.

The engineering department was detached and, as United Counties Engineering, became a direct subsidiary of the NBC.

The new United Counties retained green as the main colour in its new livery, of a shade closer to Tilling than NBC green, with cream yellow and orange stripes. In 1984, the Company carried over 49 million passengers on a mileage of almost 22 million. Compare

Above: The use of letters to denote fleet identity persisted until about 1919, after which an alphanumeric system was introduced under which the vehicles already illustrated, B and H, were renumbered A1 and A3. A5 was allocated to **LF 9970**, seen here as vehicle **J** early in its career.

Below: There is some doubt as to the identity of the coachbuilder for these early United Counties Leylands, both Birch Brothers and Christopher Dodson being possibilities. This one, identity **P**, is thought to have been registered **LH 8897** and is shown when brand new in early 1914. Later that year its chassis was commandeered by the War Department. *(Both: John Banks Collection)*

these figures with those for 1955, or even 1963, quoted above.

Deregulation and privatisation

On the last day of trading of the "old" United Counties (31st December 1985), the fleet stood at 520 vehicles; the following day the "new" Company had 263. Typical of the nonsenses spawned by the splitting up of traditional companies was that United Counties Engineering occupied premises owned by United Counties but had to compete for the business of repairing and servicing United Counties vehicles and was by no means guaranteed the work. It ceased trading in 1990.

Other effects were soon felt. In February 1986 Wellingborough depot was closed and in the April a new route network and numbering system was introduced in Northamptonshire. The need to prune the network and concentrate on "viable" routes was in part because of reduced support from the County Council. This was less of a problem in Bedfordshire and Cambridgeshire, where changes were not so severe and service numbers were not changed.

In the same year, the Coachlinks network of express services was introduced. This bold initiative covered routes, many centring on Bedford where interchange facilities were available, to and from Birmingham, Cambridge, Nottingham, London, and Luton and Heathrow Airports. Some of the routes involved were existing ones rebranded, but there were three new ones for the Coachlinks launch:

X1 Peterborough - Luton Airport via Huntingdon, St Neots and Bedford;

X2 Northampton to Luton Airport via Bedford;

X3 Cambridge to Northampton via St Neots and Bedford.

Even though claimed in Company publicity to be new, the X3 was the old 128 Northampton to Cambridge stage carriage service. The latter had suffered from a National Express two-hourly coach service between the two towns.

Deregulation Day was to come in October 1986, but the Company had introduced its "commercial" network by the end of May. Mileage registered was approximately 70% of that operated the preceding March. The national average was closer to 85%.

The 1985 Transport Act made it possible for National Bus Company operations to be sold off to the private sector. This became obligatory when the Secretary of State for Transport instructed the NBC to sell its subsidiaries by the end of January 1989. United Counties was not among the most attractive to potential private buyers. A management buy-out was unsuccessful and in November 1987 United Counties passed into the ownership of the Stagecoach group.

Afterword and acknowledgements

This book is not claimed to be either a definitive company history or a full fleet list of United Counties. To readers wishing to know more about all aspects of the Company, the excellent and comprehensive multi-part history written and published by Roger Warwick, M.C.I.T., is highly recommended. That work is replete with detail and has been of valued assistance in the production of these introductory notes. The PSV Circle fleet histories PE2 and 2PE5 have also helped, as has the *Fleet Record and Company History 1921 - 1964* published by United Counties. Thanks, too, to stalwart proofreaders Mary and Dave Shaw.

Many of the photographs were taken by G H F Atkins, among them a fine selection highlighting United Counties vehicles in Nottingham. Alan Cross, Ron Maybray and John Gillham have helped with photographs from their fine collections. Other photographic sources are individually named in the captions. The oft-encountered problem of postcards with blank backs, bought, swapped or otherwise traded over the last 40 years, means that some photographers are not known. Author and publisher offer grateful thanks to all - known and unknown - for their work in providing such a comprehensive illustration of a fascinating company.

John Banks
Romiley, Cheshire
January 2005

14

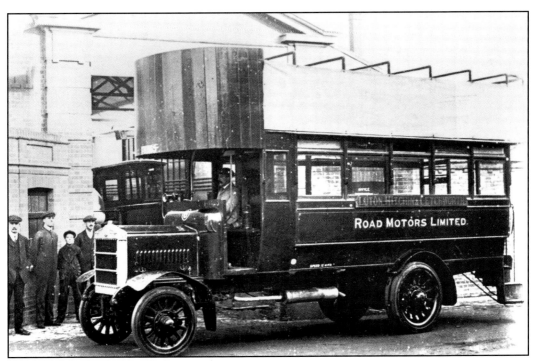

A fascinating precursor of Eastern National (and therefore of United Counties) in the Luton area was the operator Road Motors Ltd, of Luton. The link between this operator, which started work in Luton in 1912, and the later activities of United Counties in Luton, was that Road Motors established itself in premises at Langley Street, Luton, and was taken over by the National Omnibus and Transport Company in the twenties. The Langley Street garage is illustrated above, and the vehicle is Road Motors No. **6** (**FH 1165**), a circa 1917 Palladium. Palladium was a short-lived (1914-25) London manufacturer. Road Motors No. **7** (**BM 7702**), a 1919 Dennis *char-à-bancs (below)*, passed to National as No. 2245 in 1925. *(Both: John Banks Collection)*

Road Motors No. **8** (**BM 8315**) *(above)* had a Dennis 40hp chassis similar to that of No. 7 *(see page 15)*. A 1920 vehicle, it had a 31-seat body constructed by Sanders, of Hitchin, and was photographed in Dunstable when about six months old. This one also passed to National in 1925, acquiring the fleet number 2246. In the earlier part of the last century bus fleets could contain some rare *marques*. Road Motors had, in addition to the Palladium and the Dennises illustrated, at least one Milnes-Daimler and a De Dion, as well as a 20hp Federal *(below)*, which was No. **10** (**BM 9685**). The American vehicle builder Federal was in production from 1910 to 1959 and among their offerings after the 1914-8 war were several passenger vehicles with 18- to 25-seat all-metal bodies. This 1920 vehicle, however, was probably a truck chassis; its body has more than a hint of LGOC practice about it and was possibly a converted double-decker. *(Both: John Banks Collection)*

Above: Fleet number **S1** was registered **BD 3890**. It was a 1919 Leyland RAF-type chassis fitted with a lorry body later changed, in 1922, for a 52-seat double-deck bus body. It ran thus until 1929. *(John Banks Collection)*

Below: A superficially similar rebodying was carried out, in 1925, on No. **B8** (**BD 1130**), another 1919 Leyland (a 36hp model - more modern-looking than the RAF type). By the time of this early thirties photograph the vehicle had been further modernised with pneumatic tyres and windscreens and was not far from its November 1932 withdrawal. *(J F Higham/© Alan Cross Collection)*

Above: United Counties No. **A14** (**BD 4147**) was a 1920 Leyland ST type, fitted with 38-seat bodywork of unknown make. It followed the path taken by many of UCOC's early Leylands in being rebodied in the mid twenties and running for another five years or so - in this case until March 1930. *(John Banks Collection)*

Below: The solid-tyred Leylands (variously quoted as RAF5 or S4 types) purchased from United Automobile Services Ltd in July 1927 were 1922 vehicles with open-sided sightseeing bodywork. They had been used on such work in Scarborough and had originally been owned by E H Robinson of that resort, passing to United in 1926. Views of them in United Counties service are rare (they were withdrawn in 1930/1) but here is **AJ 8528** at work in Scarborough. This vehicle became UCOC No. S25 and was withdrawn in September 1930. *(John Banks Collection)*

Above: The ex-Robinson and United Leylands in new condition are epitomised by **AJ 8630**, which, when purchased by United Counties, took the fleet number S21. This one lasted in service until July 1931. *(John Banks Collection)*

Below: The move from the solid-tyred vehicles of the early twenties illustrated in the last few pictures to the pneumatic-tyred Leyland PLSC Lion of the later part of the same decade was a dramatic one. The Lion set the pattern for the standard single-deck service bus for two decades. It was immensely popular and United Counties was not slow to take advantage. Number **L20** (**RP 5971**) was a PLSC3 model (longer than the contemporary PLSC1) new in May 1928 and withdrawn by December 1939 - during which short life it was burned out and rebodied. *(J F Higham/© Alan Cross Collection)*

Above: In an Aylesbury scene circa 1932, two Leyland Lions await their departure times. The leading bus, United Counties No. **173** (**RP 6948**), a 1929 PLSC3, was bound for Winslow. The vehicle behind was another PLSC3, dating from 1928, in the Eastern National fleet. *(J F Higham/© Alan Cross Collection)*

Below: Number **L68** (**RP 7115**) was another 1929 PLSC3 Lion. It was displaying the dark-blue and white livery at Scarbrough Avenue, Skegness, in July 1929, when about three months old. It is perhaps worth explaining that at that time UCOC vehicles sometimes displayed the Company's *chassis* number, as with this vehicle, sometimes its *body* number (as with RP 6948 *above*), and sometimes *both (see page 22)*. *(G H F Atkins/© John Banks Collection)*

Above: The ride from United Counties territory to Skegness in a bus-seated Leyland Lion over the roads of the late 1920s must have been an experience. The sun was shining brilliantly on this occasion - another in July 1929 - however, and doubtless any discomforts were forgotten until the return trip. Number **L73** (**RP 7120**) was at the Lawn Motor Park in the bracing resort alongside a trio of Reos. Another superb evocation of the blue and white livery. Colour film came too late... *(G H F Atkins/© John Banks Collection)*

Below: The PLSC Lion gave way to the improved LT1 version in 1930 and - again - United Counties was quick off the mark with an order. This was among the first - perhaps *the* first: No. 193 (RP 8552) - examples, which entered service in March 1930 (this picture was taken on the 18th of that month). *(John Banks Collection)*

Leyland was also the preferred supplier for new-generation double-deckers, many of the Titan TD1 and TD2 models entering service from 1930. **RP 8564** *(above)* was a 1930 TD1; it was carrying both chassis (**4**) and body (**205**) numbers, as was 1931's No. **10/215** (**NV 10**) *(below)*. Both these Titans had Leyland 48-seat lowbridge bodywork. *(Both: J F Higham/© Alan Cross Collection)*

Above: The TD2 Titan started to enter the fleet in 1932 and the first were also Leyland-bodied 48-seaters. In 1933, however, Eastern Counties, of Lowestoft, bodied a batch as lowbridge 52-seaters. The first was No. **35/269** (**NV 2268**), seen here in as-built condition before entering service. *(Senior Transport Archive)*

Below: From about this time dual chassis and body numbers were replaced on the vehicles by a single stock number. The fleet also contained a number of second-hand Leylands, including No. **318** (**VV 693**), a 32-seat rear-entrance Duple-bodied Tiger TS3 coach dating from 1931, which came to United Counties in December 1933 with the acquisition of the Allchin & Sons, of Northampton, business. In this postwar shot the vehicle had been rebodied by Mumford, again as a 32-seater, but now with a front entrance. It had gone by the end of 1950 and was noted with the Leeds dealer W North in 1951. *(John Banks Collection)*

Upper and centre: These pictures were taken in October 1963 at Gregory Boulevard, Nottingham, at Goose Fair time. Leyland Titan TD2 **NV 1039**, formerly United Counties fleet number 243, had been new in 1932 and sold to a dealer in 1951. In 1963 it was still serving its fairground showman owner well, the Leyland lowbridge bodywork having been cut down by removal of the upper-deck windows. *(Both: G H F Atkins/© John Banks Collection)*

Lower: The Allchin & Sons acquisition also brought AECs and Daimlers, as well as oddments on Reo and Brockway chassis. AEC Regal No. **321** (**VV 696**), like the Leyland Tiger illustrated on page 23, had originally been a 32-seat rear-entrance Duple-bodied coach. In this view it had been rebodied by Mumford. *(John Banks Collection)*

Upper: Number **336** was a former Allchin Daimler CF6 fitted with Crabtree 24-seat front-entrance coachwork. Registered **NH 9227**, it lasted until September 1936 in UCOC service.

Centre: A further important acquisition, in February 1934, was of W Nightingale & Sons Ltd, of Northampton. Among a very mixed bag of vehicles were three Gilfords, of which No. **350** (**VV 498**) was one of a pair of the popular 168OT model.

Lower: The third ex-Nightingale Gilford was No. **352** (**NH 8961**), a bonneted 166SD model. This one was withdrawn in 1935, the two 168OTs a year later. *(All: J F Higham/© Alan Cross Collection)*

Above: The unusual situation whereby United Counties acquired some ex-Varsity Express Motors coaches after Eastern Counties had taken over Varsity *(see page 8)* produced some AEC Regals with coachwork by Christopher Dodson, of Willesden, typical of which was No. **375** (**VE 3032**). A 1930 machine, United Counties had it rebodied by Burlingham as a front-entrance 31-seater in 1938 and used it until 1950. *(J F Higham/© Alan Cross Collection)*

Below: Ex-Varsity and Eastern Counties No. **374** (**VE 3031**) was a similar machine with a similar history, seen here in postwar years with its 1938 Burlingham coachwork. *(W J Haynes)*

Above: Of all these second-hand acquisitions, some had less long-term potential than others, and new vehicles were also required. United Counties was in the mid thirties still an enthusiastic customer of Leyland Motors Ltd and in 1934 bought a batch of five Eastern Counties-bodied Tiger TS7 30-seat coaches, represented by No. **404** (**VV 3774**), seen at Southgate Street, Leicester, in August 1935. These fine coaches had an uneventful career and were withdrawn in 1951. *(G H F Atkins/© John Banks Collection)*

Below: Number **403** (**VV 3773**) of the same batch, seen in the early postwar period carrying a reversed colour scheme. *(John Banks Collection)*

Above: Its predeliction for Leylands notwithstanding, United Counties was now under the Tilling umbrella and group policy had to be followed, which meant the entry into the fleet of substantial numbers of Eastern Coach Works-bodied Bristols. Number **482** (**VV 6350**) was a typical example: based on the K5G chassis (signifying Gardner five-cylinder diesel power), it was new in December 1937 fitted with 55-seat lowbridge bodywork. *(Alan Cross Collection)*

Below: In the same year Bristol JO5G No. **474** (**VV 6254**), an ECW-bodied 31-seater, was put into service. *(J F Higham/© Alan Cross Collection)*

Above: The Bristol L5G succeeded the JO5G and in October 1938 United Counties took delivery of a number of 35-seat service buses. Typical of them was No. **489** (**VV 7254**), which lasted in passenger service with UCOC until June 1954.

Below: Despite the influx of Bristols, Leyland managed to win an order for a quartet of Tiger TS8s for delivery in October and November 1938. They were bodied as rear-entrance 32-seat coaches by Burlingham and were withdrawn in 1952, being sold to North, the Leeds dealer, in October of that year. The representative vehicle is No. **508** (**VV 7282**). *(Both: John Banks Collection)*

Above: The outbreak of the Second World War saw various otherwise unexpected changes to the fleet. At first, vehicles were to peacetime specification, although the choice of Roe as bodybuilder for a batch of five Bristol K5G lowbridge 55-seaters delivered in May 1940 was unusual. The batch was Nos 567-71 (BBD 811-5); they were renumbered 667-71 in March 1952 and were withdrawn in 1958. It is not known which one appears in this photograph of the type in brand new condition. *(Senior Transport Archive)*

Below: Later in the war permits had to be obtained from the Ministry of War Transport to purchase buses. Thus, in 1944, United Counties was allowed to buy three Bristol K6A (six-cylinder AEC-engined) double-deckers fitted with Strachan 55-seat lowbridge bodywork. Chassis and body were to an austere specification laid down by the Ministry of Supply. This one is No. **632** (**CBD 674**). *(John Banks Collection)*

Above: The war kept in service vehicles that otherwise might have been withdrawn and sold somewhat earlier. Many Leyland Lion PLSC models dating from the 1920s thus survived into the postwar period. PLSC3 No. **164** (**RP 6805**) still had its Leyland 35-seat body, as well as masked headlamps and white front mudguards (both aids to driving in the blackout - the one to prevent enemy bombers seeing the bus; the other to allow pedestrians to see it looming up in unlit streets). In 1946 it would be rebodied by Willowbrook and survive into the 1950s. *(John Banks Collection)*

Below: PLSC3 Lion No. **171** (**RP 6946**) followed a similar path, and here it is with its Willowbrook body, fitted in December 1945. It had also received a Bristol radiator, and only the wheel centres gave away, to the initiated, its identity as a Leyland Lion. *(Alan Cross Collection)*

Above: In 1945, the Western National Omnibus Co. Ltd, acting as agent for the Tilling companies, acquired a large batch of early Leyland Titans from Plymouth Corporation. United Counties took six, including No. **638** (**DR 9070**). A 1931 TD1, its Leyland body had been replaced with one by Beadle, to lowbridge 53-seat specification, by the time this photograph was taken on 4th April 1950. The vehicle was withdrawn in September 1954. *(Alan Cross Collection)*

Below: United Counties was not the only large company operator to buy Bedford OBs in the immediate postwar period, but the choice of Beadle bodywork was less usual. **DBD 936** was the first of a batch of six 30-seat service buses delivered in 1948. Originally No. 101, it was renumbered as 801 and then as 119. It passed via the Leeds dealer W North to Morrison, of Tenby, and by 20th April 1960, the date of this photograph in Carmarthen High Street, was running for David Jones & Son, of Ffoshelig. *(John Gillham)*

Above: Number **737** - originally 643 - (**DBD 984**) typifies early postwar deliveries from Bristol and Eastern Coach Works. A lowbridge 55-seater K5G model, it was photographed in Aylesbury on the local town service in 1961, three years or so before its November 1964 withdrawal. *(John Banks/© John Fozard Collection)*

Below: Single-deckers to the early postwar Bristol/ECW standard were also obtained in some numbers. This is 1950's No. **826** (**FRP 826**), an LL6B model (30ft-long; Bristol six-cylinder engine) that had originally been numbered 365. It was withdrawn in March 1966. *(John Banks Collection)*

Above: **FRP 822** was also of the longer Bristol LL type, but was an LL5G, fitted with a Gardner five-cylinder engine of type 5LW. Obsolete but by no means worn out when withdrawn in January 1965, it soon found further use as transport for a leisure club. It had been fleet number 822 and then 357 in the UCOC fleet. *(Ron Maybray Collection/Geoffrey Holt)*

Below: Immediately after the war, the Tilling Group set up a reconditioning programme for prewar Bristol G and J chassis. United Counties No. **430** (**NV 7497**), a 1936 Bristol JO5G, was so treated and fitted in February 1949 with an ECW 35-seat body, retaining its prewar high-mounted radiator. Regarded then as a new vehicle, it was in July 1949 despatched to Skegness, where it was photographed at the Lawn Motor Park. It was renumbered 181 in 1952 and withdrawn in 1958. *(G H F Atkins/© John Banks Collection)*

Above: Number 470 (**NV 9651**) was another prewar Bristol J to be extensively reconditioned, in this case being fitted with new frames and a lower radiator. A 1937 chassis, it was rebodied in March 1951 and renumbered **213** in 1952. Virtually indistinguishable thenceforth from a standard postwar L, it lasted in service until 1960. *(John Banks Collection)*

Below: **VV 6259**, formerly fleet numbers 461 and 204, was a similar reconditioned and rebodied prewar Bristol JO5G. After its May 1960 withdrawal it went via a dealer as staff transport for the contractor Balfour Beatty. It was photographed at Dalmally, Perthshire, on 12th September 1960. *(John Gillham)*

Above: In the late 1940s there was a brief flurry of activity involving the production of chassisless vehicles built by John C Beadle, of Dartford, using various running units. United Counties took two, with Morris-Commercial mechanicals, which were diverted from the Brighton, Hove & District Omnibus Company. The first of them, No. **168** (**FBD 915**), is seen soon after its November 1955 withdrawal. *(John Banks Collection)*

Below: **EBD 240**, a 1950 Bristol/ECW L6B 31-seat coach, had been UCOC No. 813 and then 343, and was sold to Eastern National in 1958, with whom it is seen at Harlow on excursion duties in May 1963. *(John Gillham)*

Above: The final flowering of the Bristol/ECW forward-engined coach design was the fully fronted 30ft-long 37-seater with concealed radiator. United Counties No. **835** (**FRP 835**) was an LL6B, and thus 7ft 6ins-wide. New in February 1951, it was withdrawn in 1958. The photograph was taken at Huntingdon Street bus station, Nottingham, in April 1951. *(G H F Atkins/© John Banks Collection)*

Below: The KS6B from Bristol was longer at 27ft 6ins than the 26ft K but, at 7ft 6ins, no wider. It was an interim model caught up in the flux of changing regulations governing PSV dimensions. Number **830** (**FRP 684**) was a United Counties example, originally numbered 684, that entered service in September 1950 and was withdrawn in June 1969. It was photographed at Bedford bus station on 14th July 1968 alongside UCOC Bristol Lodekka No. **604** (**WBD 604**). *(John Gillham)*

Above: After the Bristol/ECW KS model came the KSW, which was eight feet wide. These two lowbridge 55-seat examples are United Counties Nos **897** and **864** (**CNH 717** and **703**), photographed inside Luton depot in 1969. *(Ron Maybray)*

Below: Single-deckers benefited, too, from the revised regulations, which allowed 30ft-long by 8ft-wide vehicles on two axles for the first time. Bristol and ECW responded to this with the LWL, in the case of UCOC's 1952 No. **430** (**CNH 864**) with a Bristol six-cylinder engine, thus making the vehicle an LWL6B. It is seen at Stamford in August 1962. The white steering wheel was used for a time as a reminder to drivers that the vehicle was to the new maximum width. *(John Gillham)*

Above: Number **413** (**CNH 857**), another Bristol LWL6B with 39-seat ECW body, was new in January 1952. Six months later, in a rather gloomy July scene at Huntingdon Street, Nottingham, it was on front-line duties on the London express service. The Bristol AVW engine and overdrive 5th would have coped well with the run, but the service bus seats might have been found wanting by the passengers. *(G H F Atkins/© John Banks Collection)*

Below: While all these shiny new vehicles were entering service around 1950, it is noteworthy that some early-thirties Leyland Titans were still running, an example being No. **257** (**NV 1258**) of 1932. New in 1932, photographed on 4th April 1950, it would be withdrawn by the end of that year. *(Alan Cross Collection)*

Above: The shorter L model that preceded the 30ft-long Bristol LL came in several varieties, of which perhaps the most attractive was the 31-seat "dual-purpose" version of the service bus bodyshell. Typical was UCOC No. **807** (**EBD 234**), seen in June 1949 at Huntingdon Street, Nottingham, on the X1 express to London, in those days a journey of around six hours. this vehicle was transferred to South Midland Motor Services in May 1952, later passing to Thames Valley for use as a service bus.

Below: The extra length of the LL and LWL series over the L allowed an increase to 33 seats in the "dual-purpose" concept. Number **431** (**CNH 865**), with its 8ft x 30ft dimensions, might be described as representing the ultimate development of the Bristol/ECW half-cab single-decker. New in 1952, it was photographed in Howard Street, Nottingham, in June 1955. Doubtless the "1X" route number should have been "X1". *(Both: G H F Atkins/© John Banks Collection)*

Above: The great Tilling reorganisation of May 1952 in which United Counties took over the Midland Area of the Eastern National Omnibus Co. Ltd saw the Company add 247 vehicles to its fleet, which was thus not far from doubled in size. Of that total, 239 were given UCOC fleet numbers on 1st May 1952 in the new numbering system that had already seen 297 of UCOC's own vehicles renumbered on 1st March. The ex-ENOC stock included Bedford, Bristol, Dennis, Leyland and Tilling-Stevens chassis. An analysis of the transfers leaves little doubt that Eastern National arranged matters so that an unduly high proportion of older vehicles made the move to United Counties; of the many prewar units there were some that had been new in the early 1930s, including **AEV 785**, a 1933 Dennis Lancet 1 with ECOC bodywork. It took the lowest fleet number - **101** - of those allocated to ex-ENOC stock. Alongside it in this view is No. **223** (**FNO 793**), a 1937 ECW-bodied Bristol JO5G. These two vehicles were withdrawn by UCOC in 1952/3. *(Ron Maybray Collection)*

Below: Numbered in this picture as driver-trainer No. **3**, **GPU 436** was a 1938 ECW-bodied Bristol L5G, originally numbered 261 by United Counties. Although the fact will be well known to most readers, it is perhaps worth mentioning that Eastern Counties (ECOC), *as a coachbuilder*, was renamed Eastern Coach Works (ECW) in 1936, thus the two are the products of the same Lowestoft factory, formerly the coachbuilding arm of United Automobile Services. *(Ron Maybray Collection/ Geoffrey Holt)*

Above: Ex-Eastern National Leyland Titans were many and varied and comprised examples of the TD1, TD2, TD3, TD4, TD5 and PD1 models. Number **575** (**FEV 181**) was a 1937 TD5 to which ENOC had fitted a lowbridge 55-seat body in 1950. *(John Banks Collection)*

Below: **MPU 38** was still Eastern National **3977** when photographed. A 1947 ECW-bodied Titan PD1, it became United Counties No. 585. *(Ron Maybray Collection)*

Above: As might have been expected, with both ENOC and UCOC being members of the Tilling Group, standard ECW-bodied Bristol chassis, both single- and double-deck, played a large part in the transfer. Number **321** (**MPU 29**) was a 1947 L5G, which came to UCOC as a dual-purpose 31-seater. It was reseated as a 35-seat service bus in 1955 and withdrawn at the end of 1963. It was in Daventry waiting to leave for Northampton. *(Ron Maybray Collection/G Stainthorpe)*

Below: Photographed in Luton, ex-ENOC No. **735** (**MPU 19**) was a lowbridge 55-seat ECW-bodied Bristol K5G. *(Ron Maybray Collection/Geoffrey Holt)*

Above: Aylesbury was not unique as a location where standard London Transport vehicles ran cheek-by-jowl with those from the Tilling Group but it was as interesting as any, with green RTs and Green Line RFs alongside Bristol Ls and Ks. Only the RF of that quartet is missing in this scene featuring ex-Eastern National Bristol K5G No. **760** (**NNO 101**). *(Ron Maybray Collection/Geoffrey Holt)*

Below: Number **814** (**ONO 73**) was ex-Eastern National No. 4052. Another standard Bristol/ECW K5G lowbridge 55-seater, it is seen at the Market Square in Biggleswade. *(John Fozard Collection)*

Above: The more modern contingent of ex-Eastern National vehicles included No. **876** (**SHK 519**), which - as an August 1951 delivery to Eastern National - was almost new when transferred to United Counties in 1952. It was a Bristol KSW5G with 55-seat lowbridge ECW bodywork, photographed in Luton depot in 1969 not long before its March 1970 withdrawal. *(Ron Maybray)*

Below: United Counties was not alone among the company operators in having to hire vehicles in to cover shortages at peak periods. In this case, Tilling's Transport had provided 1951 ECW-bodied AEC Regal IV **LYM 732**. The 39-seater was being used on the Nottingham to London express service and was parked between runs in Howard Street, Nottingham, in April 1952. *(G H F Atkins/© John Banks Collection)*

Above: Westcliff-on-Sea No. **124** (**LHK 414**) was perhaps an even more interesting vehicle to be seen working on hire to United Counties on London express work. New to the City Coach Co. Ltd as fleet number LS3 in 1946, it was transferred to Westcliff in February 1952, when City sold its operation to the British Transport Commission, and in 1955 was absorbed into the Eastern National fleet. This picture was taken at Huntingdon Street, Nottingham, in August 1952.

Below: The early 1950s was the time of the underfloor-engined revolution, in which even quite new forward-engined half-cab vehicles were rendered obsolete overnight. The trail was blazed by Sentinel, followed by Leyland with the Olympic and the Royal Tiger, and by AEC with the Regal IV. Bristol's contribution was the LS and UCOC took a variety of bus, coach and dual-purpose versions. This one was No. **437** (**HBD 626**) a Gardner five-cylinder-engined LS5G model with 39-seat coach bodywork from Eastern Coach Works. It had run in to Skegness from Kettering in July 1954, and was parked awaiting its return timing at the Lawn Motor Park. *(Both: G H F Atkins/© John Banks Collection)*

Above: A contemporary of HBD 626 but with very different bodywork, was No. **441** (**HBD 630**). Also an LS5G, it had 43-seat service bus bodywork from ECW, but was unusual in being to the twin-doorway layout. It was converted to single front entrance in 1956, but not before it had been photographed in original condition at Huntingdon Street, Nottingham, in May 1953. Behind was a 1936 Bedford WTB, **BDK 184**, a former Yelloway vehicle by then in the fleet of Mulley's Motorways, of Ixworth in Suffolk, as fleet number 10.

Below: Another view of **HBD 630**, giving a clearer view of the original two-door arrangement. *(Both: G H F Atkins/© John Banks Collection)*

Above: A further variation on the Bristol LS5G in the UCOC fleet was the dual-purpose 39-seater based on the service-bus shell, epitomised by No. **462** (**HBD 641**), a July 1953 delivery into the United Counties fleet, seen here at Bath Street, Nottingham, in October of that year, apparently on a private hire assignment. *(G H F Atkins/© John Banks Collection)*

Below: As much a revolution in the double-deck field as the LS was in the single-deck, the Bristol Lodekka brought standard seating with a central upper-deck gangway to the low-height double-decker. Among the first United Counties examples was No. **952** (**JBD 957**), an LD6B model with 58-seat bodywork by ECW. It features in a quiet depot scene at Luton in 1969. *(Ron Maybray)*

Above: The Lodekkas began to arrive contemporaneously with deliveries of earlier-style lowbridge buses and did not oust the latter at once: some 55-seat KSW6Bs came later in 1954. The upper-deck four-in-a-row seating is just visible in this view of No. **939** (**JBD 976**) seen at Luton garage on 14th July 1968.

Below: In June 1953 United Counties took over the business and fourteen vehicles of Omar Bartle, of Potton, Bedfordshire. Not all of the vehicles were used, though all were numbered. One that was used was No. 517 (**GMJ 268**), a Weymann-bodied Guy Arab III fitted with a Gardner 5LW engine. It was withdrawn in 1956 and by August 1962 was in service with Graham's Bus Service, Paisley, as fleet number **44**. *(Both: John Gillham)*

Above: Once the new models were established, orders for new vehicles were for the underfloor-engined LS for single-deckers and the Lodekka. Number **989** (**MNV 106**) was a 1955 LD6B model with 60 seats and platform doors. It was photographed in Aylesbury about to leave for Bedford.

Below: Equally representative of the mid 1950s was the LS5G service bus with, in the case of No. **104** (**MNV 763**), 41 seats, increased to 45 in 1960. In another Aylesbury shot (the adjacent negative, in fact) the vehicle is seen on the 367 to Halton Hospital via Weston Turville. *(Both: Ron Maybray Collection/Geoffrey Holt)*

Above: Number **117** (**OBD 904**) was an example of the rarer six-cylinder Gardner-engined version of the LS - model designation LS6G. It was a 39-seat coach delivered in March 1957 and was photographed at Huntingdon Street, Nottingham, waiting its departure time for Northampton and London. *(G H F Atkins/© John Banks Collection)*

Below: By now settled as a 60-seater with platform doors, the LD6B Lodekka proliferated in the United Counties fleet in the mid to late fifties. A typical example was No. **554** (**SBD 554**), dating from March 1959, seen here leaving St Neots for Aylesbury on 23rd August 1964. *(John Gillham)*

Above: The integrally built LS model was succeeded by the MW, which reverted to separate chassis specification. An early United Counties example was 1958's No. **135 (SRP 135)**, a dual-purpose 41-seater, which was in Howard Street, Nottingham, having just worked express from London, in April 1960. The side roof-boards advertising the service are of interest.

Below: Following legislation permitting 36ft-long vehicles, Bristol produced the rear-engined RE, which was available with low and high floor levels for bus and coach work respectively. UCOC's second RE was No. **251 (ABD 251B)**, a 47-seat RELH6G model with coachwork by ECW. By now the express service, as the MX1, was using the new M1 motorway. The vehicle was at Huntingdon Street, Nottingham, in April 1964, having entered service the previous February. *(Both: G H F Atkins/© John Banks Collection)*

Above: As the times changed and officialdom permitted longer vehicles, it was natural for the Lodekka to be lengthened to 30ft, with room for 70 seats. With a forward entrance and staircase, the FLF appeared in some numbers in many Tilling fleets. This one was United Counties No. **622** (**YNV 622**), a December 1961 FLF6B, seen when still very new in a murky Aylesbury. *(John Banks)*

Below: The rear-entrance double-decker was by no means rendered obsolete by the FLF, and 27ft 6ins examples on a new variant - the FS - of the Lodekka were common. United Counties No. **676** (**DNV 676C**), an FS6B model, was a 1965 delivery, seen here in Bedford when brand new. *(Ron Maybray Collection/Geoffrey Holt)*

The FS Lodekka was among the more attractive of designs for the traditional half-cab, rear-entrance double-deck bus, and that was particularly so from the rear, revealing the coachbuilder's signature, so to speak, rather than the chassis maker's, as demonstrated by 1964's No. **671** (**CNV 671B**) in High Street, Hitchin, on 21st October 1972, and No. **668** (**CNV 668B**) at Luton in 1969. *(John Gillham; Ron Maybray)*

Upper: Number **157** (**157 BRP**) had been spotted in Victoria Coach Station by the photographer from his seventh-floor flat window (visible in the right background), causing a hurried descent, camera at the ready. A Bristol MW6G, it had been new in October 1962. *(John Banks)*

Centre: The later ECW coach body for the MW was clearly related to that for the 36ft-long RE *(see pages 52/6)* as exemplified by No. **260** (**GRP 260D**), seen at Nottingham in 1971. *(G H F Atkins/© John Banks Collection)*

Lower: In the late sixties/early seventies UCOC acquired many second-hand vehicles, including twelve Leyland Leopards with the Birch Bros business in 1969 and 77 assorted Albion, Bristol, Dennis, and Leyland vehicles in 1970 when Luton Corporation was taken over. There were also transfers from other THC operators including, in October 1968, six Bristol LS6Gs with 45-seat ECW bodies from Red and White, of Chepstow, to whom they had been new in 1953/4. UCOC No. **497** (**MAX 114**) was the last of the six. *(Senior Transport Archive)*

Above: The early United Counties RELH coaches had been painted in a version of the service bus colours, but by the time No. **264** (**KRP 264E**) came in February 1967, a reversed livery was in use. Both versions are seen in this picture, the earlier coach behind No. 264 being the first UCOC Bristol RELH, No. **250** (**250 FRP**), dating from January 1964. *(John Banks)*

Below: Mercedes-Benz O.302 demonstrator **OLH 302E** visited United Counties on loan from 5th to 22nd April 1967 and was used on the London express service via the motorway. The indefatigable Geoffrey Atkins was on hand in Nottingham to record the event. *(G H F Atkins/© John Banks Collection)*

Upper: Following the sale of the BET Group's assets to the Transport Holding Company in 1968, the way was open for the creation of the National Bus Company. The two not thereafter being in competition, a degree of cooperation in design and engineering saw the BET's curved windscreen attached to the THC's Bristol/ECW RELL bus bodyshell. The result was not unattractive, and is seen on No. **205** (**YNV 205J**), a March 1971 vehicle seen in Nottingham in the August of that year.

Centre: A less pleasing NBC change was the adoption of an allover white livery for express coaches, seen here on No. **268** (**KRP 268E**) at Nottingham Victoria in July 1975.

Lower: The transition period in early NBC days saw a great variety of liveries - here are three different ones on otherwise similar United Counties Bristol RELH coaches. *(All: G H F Atkins/ © John Banks Collection)*

Above: Here is the National white livery on a 1966 MW6G coach, No. **261** (**GRP 261D**). The arrow symbol was formed of two capital letter N graphics and the NATIONAL fleetname was in alternate blue and red letters. Having initially been banned, the subsidiary's fleetname was later allowed back, albeit in smaller script, as seen on No. 261's waistrail. *(John Banks Collection)*

Below: The rear-engined Bristol VR replaced the Lodekka in the late 1960s. Number **767** (**WRP 767J**) was an early example, with flat front, seen on private hire work at the Stoke Bruerne Canal Museum on 1st September 1963. *(John Gillham)*

A phenomenon of the last three decades of the 20th Century was the Leyland National, which appeared in many National Bus Company fleets. The first for United Counties were delivered in 1972 and many more followed. These two examples, Nos. **453** and **517** (**NBD 453M** and **OVV 517R**), dating from 1973 and 1976, were photographed working on hire to Eastern National in Chelmsford in 1986. OVV 517R was unusual in that the registration number was displayed alongside the destination screens. *(Both: Geoff Coxon)*

Above: Alexander coachwork was not common in the United Counties fleet, but the T-type 49-seat coach body appeared in 1976 on a batch of five Leyland PSU3C/4R Leopards, of which No. **225** (**MRP 225P**) is seen outside Victoria Coach Station in London in 1982.

Below: Leyland Leopards in 1977 included two PSU3E/4RT models fitted with Duple 49-seat coachwork. The first of them was No. **229** (**VRP 229S**), seen here in a 1978 photograph. *(Both: Geoff Coxon)*

Above: Five similar Leopard PSU3E/4RT chassis, again 49-seaters, appeared in January 1979, this time fitted with Plaxton Supreme Express coachwork. In another action shot near London's Victoria Coach Station, No. **236** (**EBD 236T**) is seen leaving for layover parking between express runs.

Below: Similar chassis in 1980, again as a batch of five, had Willowbrook 003 Mk II coachwork, as before of 49-seat capacity. In a 1982 view, at the opposite side of Victoria Coach Station, No. **241** (**KVV 241V**) is illustrated. *(Both: Geoff Coxon)*

Above: Although orders for coaches were routinely going to Leyland, United Counties was still ordering double-deckers from Bristol into the 1980s. Number **957** (**VVV 957W**), new in April 1981, is seen in a livery for Interlink Parcels. It passed, still in this livery, to Luton & District in the January 1986 split.

Below: Smaller capacity buses in 1981 were three Lex-bodied 33-seat Bedford YMQS models, represented by No. **51** (**WNH 51W**) in a 1982 photograph. All three also went to Luton & District in January 1986. *(Both: Geoff Coxon)*

Above: The successor to the Bristol VR, and a project to which Bristol Commercial Vehicles had contributed much, was the Leyland Olympian - the first examples, indeed, were built at Bristol before Leyland closed that factory down. The last United Counties VRs came in June 1981, and the first Olympians in the August, although No. **620** (**ARP 620X**) was a January 1982 arrival.

Below: Among the Leyland Leopards delivered in 1982 were eight PSU3F/4R models with Eastern Coach Works 49-seat bodies which came in March. The first of them, No. **170** (**CNH 170X**), is seen in London later in 1982. *(Both: Geoff Coxon)*

Above: The January 1986 split saw 1981 Leyland Leopard No. **156** (**VNH 156W**) transferred to the new Milton Keynes City Bus Ltd. The 49-seat coachwork was by Duple to their Dominant design.

Lower: Number **120** (**C120 PNV**), in a 1986 photograph, shows the new white and blue-grey Coachlinks livery. The Leyland Tiger chassis was carrying Plaxton Paramount coachwork. *(Both: Geoff Coxon)*